THE
RIVER NIAGARA.

FORT NIAGARA — 1812.

"Truth is stranger than fiction."

THE
RIVER NIAGARA.

DESCRIPTIVE
AND
HISTORICAL.

PAN-AMERICAN EDITION.

By BARTON ATKINS

BUFFALO, N.Y.
1899.

MADE IN
THE COMPLETE ART-PRINTING WORKS
OF
MATTHEW-NORTHRUP CO.
BUFFALO, N. Y.
18986

Media Hatchery
Orchard Park, NY

All text and illustrations in this publication are in the public domain and were obtained from the Library of Congress. All other text, design, and formatting are
© 2021 by William C. Even — Media Hatchery.

All rights reserved.

ISBN: 978-0-9971276-8-3 (Paperback Edition)

Front cover illustration:
Niagara, river and cantilever bridge (ca. 1900),
photomechanical print, Detroit Publishing Company.
Obtained from the Library of Congress
Prints and Photographs Division.

Printed and bound in the United States of America
First Printing 2021

Published by Media Hatchery
P. O. Box 554
Orchard Park, NY 14127

MediaHatchery.com

DEDICATION.

To my mother, Mary Jane. The mere fact that I survived my childhood and am still alive to write this dedication speaks volumes of her infinite patience and love.

— W. C. Even

The River Niagara.

CHAPTER I.

EARLY HISTORY.

THE Pan-American Exposition is located on the border of the most wonderful and renowned fresh-water course on the globe. The eventful history of the Niagara River is in keeping with majestic wonders of Nature there presented.

The wonderful Niagara! flowing from Lake Erie to Lake Ontario, prior to 1825 (when was opened the Erie Canal), was the gateway to western empire and civilization, a prominent factor in the settlement of a region now of vast expanse and population, and of unlimited resources. This writing is descriptive of the famous river, of its historic localities, and of the important events occurring thereon and thereby, on the march to civilization and settlement.

The region was first known to the civilized world through the report of James Cartier, a French navigator, who, in 1534, discovered and explored the Gulf of St. Lawrence.

Cartier was told, by the natives, that the big river flowing into the Gulf came from a big lake far in the interior, and the end of the lake, another big river flowed therein, and in that river was a mighty waterfall, but beyond that, they knew nothing. Cartier explored the St. Lawrence, before returning to France, as far as the present city of Montreal; and in his report to his government is first mentioned the existence of the river Niagara and its cataract — so far as history tells.

The River Niagara.

The disclosures of Cartier stimulated the zeal of Jesuit missionaries and fur-traders, who, after a long interval, penetrated the vast water course and the wilderness adjacent thereto. Prior to the close of the sixteenth century, these adventurers were established on the lower St. Lawrence, and early in the seventeenth century Champlain, on the borders of Lake Ontario, was warring the native Iroquois, in order establish the colony of New France. In 1669 came the intrepid explorer, Robert Cavelier de La Salle, who penetrated Lake Ontario unto its western extremity, to Burlington Bay, where he held a conference with the Indians, on the spot where is now the City of Hamilton. From thence La Salle returned easterly, to the mouth of the Genesee River, through which water course he crossed the present State of New York, and beyond, reaching a "large river," supposed have been the Ohio.

La Salle's account of that expedition does not state that he then entered *The River Niagara*.

Ten years later, La Salle returned to Lake Ontario, and on a small vessel of ten tons, sailed into the mouth of the big river, called by the natives Niah-gaah. Such orthography was changed to Niagara by the French, in 1688. History does record that white men entered the River prior to La Salle.

The little vessel ascended the river for seven miles, unto the lower rapids, where her progress was interrupted. At the foot of the rapids, on the east bank of the river, La Salle constructed a cabin surrounded by a palisade, a store house — his base of supplies for his projected expedition to explore the great inland waters beyond. La Salle's structure was erected where is now Lewiston Landing, and the locality has the distinction of being the first foothold of white men on the borders of the Niagara.

With La Salle was Father Hennepin, who made an exploration of the river unto Lake Erie, and gave to history the first description of the great cataract thereon. The river is believed to have been traversed by Jesuit missionaries as early as 1640, though no account thereof was made known to history.

Five miles above the cataract La Salle constructed a larger vessel, the historic *Griffon*, with which he and Hennepin, on August 7, 1679, sailed into Lake Erie; the first vessel, other than canoes, and, perhaps, the batteaux of the missionaries, to float on the great waters above the Falls of Niagara.

The Niagara Frontier, in early time, was a dark and bloody ground of savage warfare. The region was for a long period peaceably occupied by the Neuter Nation, but the more powerful nation of Iroquois coveted their grand hunting and fishing ground, and, to obtain possession thereof, waged a war of extermination against the occupants, ending with their utter annihilation.

Later on the region was the scene of bloody strife between the forces of France and England, each with savage allies, in furtherance of their frantic schemes of American colonization; and, subsequently, of the heroic battles between American and British forces in the war of 1812.

CHAPTER II.

THE RIVER AND ISLANDS.

IN its immense water-flow, its grand scenery and historic lore, the Niagara is one of the most renowned rivers of the world. The single outlet of the great inland seas: lakes Superior, Huron, Michigan, St. Clair and Erie, together with their hundreds of tributary streams, comprising a water surface of 500,000 square miles, more than one-half the fresh water of the globe, must justify such distinction. On its course from Lake Erie, for three miles, the river is only one-half mile in width, varying in depth from twenty to forty feet, and with a current flowing nine miles per hour over a rock bottom. At the end of this distance the shores recede, until reaching a width (measuring across Grand Island) of eight miles from shore to shore. Here the flow of waters is more peaceful, yet diligently the large volume glides along to its precipitous leap. Two miles above the Falls, where the river is about two miles wide, the flood of waters commence, between contracting shores, a wild rush for the cataract, thus increasing its velocity to fifteen miles per hour before taking its awful plunge. From that point to the verge of the falls, the descent is fifty-seven feet, and then a perpendicular fall of 164 feet into the boiling abyss below. These two miles of rapids are an important feature of the wonders of Niagara, the foam-crested breakers dashing and leap-

The River and Islands.

Niagara Falls.—From a Sketch Made in 1795.

ing twenty the main current. The raging waters roar, hiss and boil in endless agony, a scene awing to the beholder.

The two views of the Falls herein displayed are of ancient origin, being taken from a sketch made in 1795, by Duke de Liancourt, a French savant, then a pilgrim to Niagara. His description of the cataract is quaint reading. An extract is appended:

"There it falls one dense awful mass of green waters, unbroken and resistless; here it is broken into drops, and falls like a sea of diamonds sparkling in the sun. Now it shoots forth like rockets in endless succession, and now it is so light and foaming that it dances in the sun as it goes. Then there is the deep expanding pool below, where the waters pitch in agitation and foam, and beyond the waters spread out like a rippling sea of alabaster.

"This last feature is perfectly unique, and one would think nothing could add to its loveliness; but there lies upon it, as if they were made for each other, 'Heaven's own bow.' O, never in heaven itself had it so fair a resting place.

"Above and overhanging me was Table Rock, while immediately before me was spread, in all its height and majesty, the unspeakable cataract itself; seeming to fall direct from heaven, and rushing to the earth with a weight and voice that made the rocks around me fairly tremble. The power, the sublimity, the beauty, the bliss of the scene — it cannot be told."

Some three score years ago a pilgrim to Niagara was inspired in manner partially as follows:

> Hail! thee — Colossal Flood! thy majesty and might
> Amazes — then enraptures — then o'erawes the sight;
> The glare of lordly kings, in every clime and zone,
> Is dim beneath the splendor of thy o'erpour'ng throne.
> No hindrance to thy lusty flow, no power bids thee stay,
> Onward — ever onward — thy current holds its way;
> The rising mists that veil thee — thy grand overpour,

Proclaim thee — Creation's Wonder! with an endless roar.
Thy diadem — an emerald green — of the rarest, purest hue,
Set on waves of snowy foam and spray of fleeting dew;
Tresses of the brightest pearls adorn thy stately sheet,
The rainbow lays its radiant gems in homage at thy feet.

* * * * * *

If mountains are as naught in the hollow of Thy hand,
If continents, in Thy balance, are but grains of sand;
If Niagara is so very great, to us who lowly bow,
O, Creator! of all, how surpassing great art Thou!

For seven miles below the Falls the river courses through a deep gorge, about 800 feet wide, lined by towering walls, the tops of which are on a level with the river banks above the cataracts. At the foot of the gorge is Lewiston, where the river again expands, and from thence peacefully flows seven miles further to Lake Ontario. For nearly two miles below the Falls the current is sluggish, with a depth of 250 feet. Then, again, the flood rushes on with appalling velocity down channel, between high walls, not more than 700 feet wide at several points. The sublime grandeur of the scene confuses human comprehension. When gazing upon the angry flood through this portion of the gorge, an unequaled scene is presented. At some points in its mad rush, the pent-up current piles up in the middle of the stream, nine feet higher than at the edge. Nowhere in the world are waters more turbulent.

"------------------------impetuously,
The raging waters sweep;
They come in their sublimity,
Descending leap o'er leap.
In wrath and roar they rush along,
Through cragged rocks they flow;
Madly roaring down it comes,
It boils, and foams, and thunders through."

GORGE RAPIDS.—From a Photograph.

The descent of the river from Lake Erie to Lewiston, seven miles below the Falls, is about 336 feet. From the lake to the cataract, the descent is eighty-seven feet; then a perpendicular fall of 164 feet; front thence, through the gorge to Lewiston, seven miles, the fall is about eighty-six feet. When contemplating the vast source of water supply, the immensity of the flow will be justified. Of the quantity of water passing over the Falls, estimates have been made by several scientists. Professor Lyell says, fifteen hundred millions of cubic feet every minute. Dr. Dwight estimates that over one hundred millions of tons over the horseshoe fall every hour.

It is estimated that at the center of the horseshoe cataract, and for distance above, the water is at least twenty feet deep. Such estimate was confirmed in 1829, when the schooner *Detroit* passed over that point. The bottom of the vessel was broken in the rapids above, when the hull became water-logged, and sunken decks to, necessarily drawing eighteen feet. Nevertheless, for a distance above, and over the brink, the wreck met no obstruction, passing freely over. The *Detroit* was a prize of Perry's victory! Having been naturalized amid the booming of big guns, she served as an American merchantman some fifteen years, and then was sold for an exhibition.

The islands of the river, including islets in the rapids above the cataracts, are about forty in number. First in course is Squaw Island, containing 131 acres; then Strawberry Island, about 100 acres. Then comes Grand Island, commencing five miles below Lake Erie, and extending to within three miles of the Falls, containing 17,384 acres of well-timbered and productive land. Flanking Grand Island are Beaver Island, thirty acres Rattlesnake, forty-five acres; Buckhorn, 145 acres; Tonawanda Island, sixty acres; and Navy Island, 300 acres. Below, near the American shore, is Cayuga Island, 100 acres. Of these, Beaver, Navy and Cayuga are timbered, and have good soil.

THE HORSESHOE CATARACT, CANADIAN SIDE.—From a Sketch Made in 1795.

Goat, properly Iris, Island divides the Falls into separate sheets. It is about half a mile long, and about half the distance in width; containing seventy-five acres of timbered land. Situated between channels of wild rapids, and flanked on either side by the most majestic cataracts in the world, it is, beyond question, the most picturesque, fascinating and romantic spot of earth on the globe. Visitors are reluctant to depart therefrom, and are wont to muse with Montgomery:

> "If God hath made this world so fair,
>   Where sin and death abound;
> How beautiful beyond compare,
>   Will Paradise! be found."

CHAPTER III.

HISTORIC POINTS.

Fort Niagara was originally constructed as a defensive work, in 1686, by the Marquis De Nonville, a French military officer. La Salle erected two block-houses on the site in 1678, which, however, were burned soon after. The fortification has in turn been occupied by the French, English and Americans. Some of the ancient structures erected by the French still exist. The location is one of the most beautiful and eligible for the purpose in all America. In the promotion of western discovery, civilization and settlement, as a base, the fort was of great importance; and during two centuries of time it was coveted in war, and in intrigue with the native savages.

Opposite Niagara is the pleasant village of Niagara-on-the-Lake, once called Newark; and a short distance above, on the river bank, is Fort George, a defensive work constructed in 1798. Fort George was besieged and captured by the Americans in 1813. Six miles above, on the Canadian side, is Queenston, where a desperate battle between British and American forces was fought, July 25, 1814. In this engagement the British General Brock, a valorous officer, was killed. There, on a bold prominence, stands his majestic monument, visible from many miles surrounding. This shore is hallowed ground. In fact, the west bank of the river, all the way to Fort Erie, is extremely picturesque and interestingly historic. Over this highway both armies of the war of 1812 marched and countermarched to the strains of martial music, each, in turn, to triumph, and on retreat. On the American side, opposite Queenston, is Lewiston, celebrated as the white man's first foothold on the Niagara Frontier above Lake Ontario.

Three miles above Lewiston is the Devils Hole, a deep gorge, penetrating, at right angles, the high wall of the river. It is 150 feet deep, with perpendicular walls. Here, in 1763, was enacted a horrible tragedy. A wagon-train conveying military supplies, consisting of twenty or more wagons, was attacked by five or six hundred Indians, who pillaged the train and threw the horses, oxen and wagons over the bank, and massacred all but two of the drivers and escorts. Hearing of the affray, the garrison at Lewiston, consisting of two companies of troops, hastened to the scene. On their arrival the savages were in ambush, and all but a half dozen of the soldiers were killed, some by musket balls, some by the tomahawk, and some by being driven over the bank to certain death on the bottom rocks. Eighty scalps were the trophies of the savages.

Three miles above the cataract, on the American shore, is the historic landing, Fort Schlosser, originally named Fort du Page, by the French, and subsequently, Little Fort, by the British, and was given its modern name, for Captain Joseph Schlosser, a German serving in the British army on the frontier, in 1759. The landing is further noted as the place where the steamboat *Caroline* was cut out and sent flaming over the Falls, December 29, 1837. The locality is now the site of extensive electric works, and named Echota.

On the opposite shore, abreast of Fort Schlosser, is the quaint town of Chippewa, a noted battleground of the war of 1812. The village contains a number of old buildings erected in the eighteenth century.

On the American shore, under the shelter of Cayuga Island, in 1679, La Salle constructed the *Griffon*, the pioneer vessel of western civilization. The river and island scenery there presented is yet the same as when the historic vessel was launched 220 years ago.

Still another famous locality is Perry's Shipyard, under the shelter of Squaw Island. Here, in 1813, were constructed three vessels, to add to the fleet building at Presque Isle.

The old ferry to Fort Erie was an early enterprise. Early voyagers mentioned its existence at the time of the Revolution. Until the advent of the horseboat, in 1825, the ferry was supplied with scows propelled by sweeps, wielded by lusty watermen.

The illustration, a reproduction of an old print published in 1816, shows the landing on the American side, where now is the Front.

An historic institution is the ferry across the Niagara to Fort Erie. Could it relate its history, interesting interviews would be in order.

Historic Points.

The Old Ferry Landing.—Prior to 1825

CHAPTER IV.

THE WAR AT BUFFALO.

ON June 26, 1812, a messenger from Washington arrived on the frontier with intelligence that war had been declared against Great Britain. The American schooner *Connecticut*, in ignorance of the fact, was then at anchor off the mouth of Buffalo Creek, awaiting a fair wind to depart up the lake. In the afternoon the schooner was approached by two rowboats filled with armed Canadians, who seized the vessel and moved her to a position covered by the guns of Fort Erie.

This was the first hostile demonstration of the war on the Niagara frontier. Then, batteries and earthworks were thrown up on both banks of the river. Above the mouth of Scajaquada Creek was the Sailors' Battery, where were mounted three 32-pounders. One-half mile above this was another battery of three guns. Below the present site of Fort Porter was Fort Tompkins, a larger fortification. Just above Fort Tompkins was a mortar battery, armed with an eight-inch mortar. This historic implement of war now poses, fitly inscribed, near the monument in Lafayette Park; accompanied by two British cannon captured with the brig *Adams*, in a conflict hereafter described. On the ninth of October, Lieut. Elliott, a naval officer assigned to the frontier with Perry, stood on the river bank, where now is Fort Porter, watching a vessel approaching from the lake. Near by Elliott stood the famous Seneca Chief, Farmers Brother, also with eyes on the vessel.

Then the new arrival anchored nigh unto the British brig-of-war *Adams*, moored under the guns of Fort Erie. The stranger was the British schooner *Caledonia*, with a cargo of furs from Lake Huron. Farmers Brother, ever loyal to the Americans, said to Elliott, when pointing to the two vessels, "You take 'em, got furs, plenty. You take boats, soldiers, plenty, night, dark, you take 'em."

The lieutenant grasped the suggestion of the old chief with enthusiasm, and at once took action. Applying to Capt. Towson of the army for a force of men, that officer readily entered into the scheme. At one o'clock in the morning four boats, filled with armed men, left the American shore, two under the direction of Towson, and the two others under Elliott. The night was rainy and dark. Making a detour well above the unsuspecting enemy, they allowed the boats to silently drift down the current upon the vessels. Simultaneously they were boarded, and before their sleeping force was half awakened the Americans had possession of the vessels, had slipt their cables, and had them under sail for the American shore. Fifty-eight prisoners were captured, including three officers; and thirty-eight American prisoners, confined on the brig *Adams*, were recaptured. With the expedition were three citizen volunteers: Dr. Cyrenius Chapin, Guy J. Atkins and James Sloan. The two latter navigated the vessels after their capture.

In 1812 Buffalo was a frontier hamlet of about 500 people, and one hundred buildings. These were scattered along on what is now Main Street from the Terrace up to the present Goodell Street. Then the Terrace was a sandy bluff, between which and the creek stretched a morass with a riotous growth of bushes and rank grasses. The lake, river, and Canada shore at Fort Erie were in plain view from the sand bluff. From other directions a dense forest crowded the hamlet.

When war came it brought dire calamity to the village of Buffalo. Its inhabitants were compelled to flee from the flames of their burning homes in mid-winter to find shelter in adjacent settlements. With the exception of two buildings, their village was in ashes. The following account of the burning, recently published for the first time, is a concise and conservative statement:

"When Gen. Wilkinson, in 1813, retired to lower Lake Ontario, he left Gen. McClure in command of the force on the Niagara, who made his headquarters at Fort George, from whence he issued flaming proclamations, and when abandoning that position committed the needless cruelty of burning the adjacent village of Newark, thereby turning helpless families out into winter's cold and snow. The inhuman act brought condign punishment on the American frontier. Then McClure took up headquarters in Buffalo. The British, fired with the spirit of revenge, undertook reprisals. The whole riverside from Lewiston to Tonawanda Creek was devastated by the British and their allied savages. During the three weeks following the destruction of Newark, six American villages were burned, together with all the scattered homes the avengers could find. Gen. McClure called for volunteers to rally for the defense of Buffalo, and then went to Batavia and gave up the command to Gen. Hall, who hurried on to Buffalo such available force as he could find, where he arrived December 25th, and did all he could to repel the invaders. The tale has often been told how small detachments of Americans were in turn thrown against the enemy, and in turn demoralized; how the British landed at Black Rock and marched up to the doomed village, dispersing such resistance as they met. Then followed a scene which passes description. The few roads leading out from the burning hamlet were thronged with a motley crowd, all hurrying as fast as possible from the revengeful enemy, with terror blanching every face."

Such was the result of the unnecessary destruction of the Canadian village by Gen. McClure on his evacuation of Fort George; and who then and there disgraced the uniform of an American officer in so doing. A true soldier would have shrunk from such wanton cruelty.

CHAPTER V.

BATTLE OF SCAJAQUADA CREEK.

IN the summer of 1814, Fort Erie was garrisoned by American troops, under Brig.-Gen. Gains. On August 3d, Gen. Drummond marched his British regulars, 3,000 strong, from the garrisons at Chippewa and Fort George, up the west bank of the Niagara, to storm the fort. On his arrival, the British commander learned that the works were manned secure against a *coup de main*, which caused him to resort to an investment. An expedition to seize military stores, and destroy magazines at Buffalo, consisting of a strong force under Col. Tucker, was thrown across the river, landing below the mouth of Scajaquada Creek, with orders to cross before daybreak, and then strike for the supplies and magazines. Gen. Brown, anticipating such a purpose, had withdrawn Maj. Morgan, with his force of riflemen, from Fort Erie, and had them stationed at Black Rock, to watch the movements of the enemy. Morgan descried the British approaching, and moved his men to the south bank of the Scajaquada, removed the planking from the bridge spanning the stream, and there awaited the enemy.

When the raiding force arrived they found the bridge of no avail, and the stream unfordable.

When attempting to repair the bridge, the enemy received a warm reception from the riflemen, causing them to fall back on the line, and then, for upwards of an hour, a hot battle ensued.

In the mean time Tucker had dispatched a strong force on a left flank, to ford the creek higher up stream. Morgan met this force at the ford with a like detachment, where a fierce combat took place, ending with the recoil of the enemy, and retirement to their main body.

Having in two attempts failed to cross the creek, the enemy gathered their dead and wounded and hastily retreated to their boats, and returned to the west side of the river.

There were a number of sharp encounters on the banks of the Scajaquada during the war, the above described being the last of the series — the farewell engagement.

The Scajaquada! The historic water-course named for an historic chieftain; whose lone cabin marked its bank prior to the footprints of the white man. The word is of Iroquois dialect and signifies isolation — "away from the multitude." Reverently the stream observes simplicity, as yet, its loneliness is unbroken, quietly it winds the monumental slopes of Forest Lawn. Then, on its way to the Niagara, it courses the picturesque grounds of the Pan-American Exposition.

CHAPTER VI.

THE SIEGE OF FORT ERIE.

THE account here given of the battles of Fort Erie is based on the reports to Congress of the then Secretary of War, December, 1814. On the 12th of August, Gen. Drummond's defensive and offensive measures being completed, he, on the morning of the 13th, began his attack on the fort by a heavy cannonade. This was continued until the evening of the 14th, without material damage to the works.

The American commandant concluded that an assault would be made during the night, it being rainy and very dark. Accordingly, he made such disposition of his comparatively small force, as would best enable him to repel it.

About two o'clock in the morning a heavy column of the enemy was found approaching Towson's battery, when the well directed discharges therefrom, aided by a shower of musketry, compelled the British to fall back. A second attempt on the same point met a like result. Then the enemy made a flank movement on the water side of the fort, and here the movable part of the defence, under Wood and Ripley, met the attack and decisively repulsed it, the falling enemy drifting away with the current — those who were wading the stream. At this juncture, the enemy's central column was pressing forward on the line of entrenchment connecting the batteries of Towson and Williams; but, though making vigorous effort, they were checked by the fire of Biddle's and Fanning's artillery, sustained by a regiment of rifles, and Porter's volunteers.

While such were the failures of the enemy, in the next assault, after two repulses in which the enemy suffered great loss, they at last got possession of this, one of the outer bastions of the fort. The enemy's force first entering the bastion was led by Col. Drummond, a relative of the general in command, a brave, but inhuman officer. As the enemy rushed in, Drummond, who was in the lead, shouted "Charge, give the Yankees no quarter." His followers rushed upon the Americans and a hand-to-hand conflict ensued. Williams and Macdonough were wounded. They asked for quarter, but Drummond refused, emptying his pistol into Macdonough's body. Then an American infantryman, who witnessed the act, shot Drummond through the heart, and he was a dead man, while his victim, Macdonough, yet lingered in life. A few moments later a terrific explosion occurred within the bastion occupied by the enemy, blowing the structure into the air, and killing or maiming most of those inside. The cause of the explosion was generally attributed to the dying Macdonough, who, to avenge his wanton murder, threw a torch into a large magazine chest standing near where he was shot down. Soon after the explosion, the enemy retired to their entrenchments, and the combat ended; but leaving on the field 220 dead and 174 wounded; 186 of the enemy were made prisoners. Though defeated his attempt to the fort by storm, the British commander, adhering to his purpose of reducing it, opening new trenches, and establishing additional batteries.

At the battle of Lundy's Lane, in July previous, Gen. Brown and Gen. Scott were wounded. Gen. Brown had so far recovered from his wound that he hastened to Fort Erie, and again, on the 2d of September, assumed command of the American forces on the frontier.

During four weeks ensuing, both combatants were strengthening their positions, and augmenting their forces for the final struggle. The enemy had been materially reinforced, and had constructed additional batteries and trenches. The Americans were reinforced by a column of militia recruited in Buffalo by Gen. Porter. The enemy delaying an attack, Gen. Brown, though with an inferior force, determined to storm the enemy's position according to plans submitted by Gen. Porter.

On the 18th, the Americans were formed into double columns of attack; that of the left, composed of Porter's volunteers, Gibson's riflemen, and the remains of the 1st and 23d regiments of infantry was marched through a wood, and flanked the enemy's right; while that of the American right, under Brig.-Gen. Miller, made up of the remains of the 9th, 11th, 17th, 19th, and 21st regiments of infantry, took position on the western front of the enemy, with orders to force his entrenchments between batteries Nos. 2 and 3. Such orders were promptly executed by the gallant Miller, and in a time remarkably short, three batteries of the enemy, two block houses and their connecting intrenchments, were captured and destroyed.

In producing this result, the column led by Wood, Porter and Gibson had their full share of the work. After turning the enemy's right, it carried by storm a strong block house in rear of battery No. 3; spiked, in the latter, three 24-pounders, blew up the magazine, and then assisted Miller in reducing battery No. 2.

"It was thus," reported Gen. Brown, "that in a close action, not exceeding an hour's time, one thousand troops of the line, and an equal number of New York militia, routed the enemy, and diminished his effective force one thousand men. An attack so bold in its conception could not be made without severe loss; amounting in the aggregate to 511 men, including officers and privates. Among the officers killed were the gallant intrepids, Wood and Gibson.

Then Gen. Drummond, with the remnant of his division, made a hasty retreat to Fort George. The enemy's loss in killed, wounded, and prisoners captured was upwards of one thousand, officers and men.

Thus were contested the obstinate battles of Fort Erie. The sanguinary conflicts at Queenston, Chippewa and Lundy's Lane are equally rated in history as among the most desperate engagements between armed men in the annals of modern warfare.

The visitor at Buffalo, when viewing its picturesque waterfront, can gaze upon the broad expanse of Lake Erie, the turbulent flow of the Niagara, and, where lake and river join, can see the ruins of Fort Erie; and, below, the beautiful landscape of the Canadian shore for miles in extent. In fact, nowhere else in the world, within the distance, are Nature's wonders so bountifully displayed; nowhere are spots of earth, in western history, more historic, than are the borders of the Niagara River.

The River Niagara.

View of Buffalo: Looking Through the Ruins of Fort Erie.

CHAPTER VII.

THE PATRIOT WAR.

WITHIN a few months after the final battle of Fort Erie the war was at an end, and there after the angel of peace proclaimed her victories on the frontier for a long period — until 1837, when the Canadian people were in trouble with an uprising factious partisans in rebellion against their local government. Under their leader, McKenzie, the self-styled "Patriots" congregated in large numbers on the American border, and early in the winter occupied Navy Island, in the Niagara River, which is British soil. There, with the loyalists on the opposite Canadian shore, they maintained an artillery duel for several weeks. The main casualty of the engagement was on the island, where a cannon-shot penetrated the head of one man and a barrel beans, of causing a wild scattering of brains and beans — principally beans.

The winter of 1837-8 was an open one, there being no ice in lake or harbor at Buffalo prior to late in January. The little river steamboat *Caroline* had a enjoyed quiet Christmas moored in the harbor, when her owner conceived the brilliant idea that his boat could "earn her board" plying between Fort Schlosser and the rebel camp on Navy Island. Accordingly, on the early morn of December 28th the *Caroline*, gaily decorated with bunting, and carrying a score or more of curious sightseers, steamed out of the harbor and hied herself down the

The River Niagara.

Niagara to Fort Schlosser. During the afternoon the boat made two round trips to Navy Island, and then, in fancied security, tied up for the night at Schlosser dock, with the party curios, including her owner, camped in the little cabin below deck. About two o'clock in the morning the boat was boarded by a party of loyalists from Canada, her sleeping party aroused, and, in their night clothes, hustled onto the wharf; the boat was cast off, fired, set adrift, and in flames she went kiting over the Falls; carrying therewith the nether garments of the sightseers from Buffalo, together with an unpaid board bill. One of the curios, a man named Duffee, an American citizen, who objected to the proceeding, and refused to walk ashore, was promptly killed and his body thrown onto the wharf.

Then the pot boiled on the American side: "An American vessel cut out of a home port, a citizen murdered and the property of a citizen destroyed," raised a flurry of indignation all along the border. The excitable event became the subject of considerable argument with the English Government. On their part it was claimed that the boat had forfeited her neutrality; had aided the insurgents, in conveying to them arms and supplies; and that when arrested on the scene, wherever found, her seizure was justifiable. Such claim was confirmed by the United States on the trial of one of the raiders, who subsequently was arrested when visiting this side, and indicted for murder, tried and acquitted. However, the British government made a courteous apology, when the matter was dropped and soon forgotten.

CHAPTER VIII.

GEN. SCOTT AND COL. KIRBY.

WHEN occupying Navy Island, the Patriots burglarized the State arsenal at Batavia, and took therefrom a quantity of war material belonging to the State of New York, and conveyed the same to the island.

This event, and the affair of the *Caroline*, brought Gen. Scott of the army and William L. Marcy, Governor of the State, to Buffalo. In the latter part of January, 1838, the insurgents evacuated Navy Island, leaving thereon the property stolen from the State of New York. Gov. Marcy chartered the steamboat *Barcelona* to go to the island and recover the property, the State guaranteeing safety to the boat in the undertaking. In the early morning the little steamer passed down the river, landing at Black Rock to take on a military force assigned from Fort Porter. Col. Kirby, the Canadian officer of customs, concluded to interrupt and confiscate the offending boat on her return up the river; he considering her equally as culpable as was the *Caroline*. Opportunely, two armed Canadian schooners were moored at Waterloo, opposite Black Rock, which were Col. Kirby's means and a strong wind up the river his opportunity. About midday the armed vessels were anchored in mid-stream awaiting the return of the *Barcelona*. Gen. Scott was on the ground and had ordered two 24-pounders placed on the river bank abreast of the belligerent vessels. Then two men rowed out to the schooners from the American shore, conveying a message from Gen. Scott to Col. Kirby, stating that the *Barcelona* was an American vessel engaged in a lawful undertaking, and that if she was fired upon, or otherwise illegally interrupted on her passage up the river, that he, Gen. Scott, would sink both vessels, with shots from an American battery.

Both banks of the river were lined with expectant and excited people. The cannon were charged and the gunners were at their station. A like situation was revealed by field glasses to be in order on the schooners. All eyes were cast down stream for the expectant steamboat. About sundown she was sighted stemming the current. Slowly she approached, while all hearts throbbed excitedly. Finally, the steamer lapped the schooners, yet, not a gun was fired, not a funeral note was heard, as up the rapids she paddled. Then the vessels weighed anchor and dropped into their moorings at Waterloo, and the game of bluff between Col. Kirby and Gen. Scott was at an end. They had met before — at Chippewa and Lundy's Lane.

Gen. Scott and Col. Kirby.

The Walk-in-the-Water, 1818. — From a Sketch by Ebenezer Walden, 1818.

CHAPTER IX.

THE ORIGINAL WESTERN STEAMBOAT.

INTO the Niagara River, in 1818, was launched the first steamboat known to the western empire. There, under the shelter of Squaw Island, was built the steamboat *Walk-in-the-Water*, and on August 25th, following, she started on her first passage over the surface of Lake Erie, bound for Erie, Cleveland, Sandusky and Detroit. On this course she developed a speed of above seven miles per hour, which was considered a complete success.

Thus eighty years ago Lake Erie was navigated by a single steam craft. Now, the steam tonnage entering the port of Buffalo, during the season of lake navigation, is greater than like entries of any other port of the world. Such facts illustrate the wonderful progress of western civilization and settlement, the first march of which was through the river Niagara.

The first Lake Erie steamboat was built on the spot of ground where were constructed three vessels of the fleet with which Commodore Perry fought and won the naval battle of Lake Erie, September 10, 1813. The main portion of the fleet was built at Presque Isle, now Erie. The illustration here presented is a reproduction of 1816, claimed by the original publisher to have been from a sketch of the commodore, taken on the spot.

The Original Western Steamboat.

Perry's Shipyard. — Presque Isle, 1813. — From an Old Print.

CONCLUSION.

Such is the world-renowned Niagara River, and such were the historic happenings thereon and thereby. Visitors to the Pan-American Exposition will have ample facilities to visit its every point. All is hallowed ground. Excursion steamers and steam yachts ply briskly o'er its navigable waters, while steam cars, and cars driven by electricity engendered by the mighty cataract, whirl over its shores from lake to lake.

The Niagara is a paradise for the angler. A prize capture is a lusty bass taken from the swift transparent current. Ye Gods!

BUFFALO.

Where flaming swords were in anger drew,
Where Red Jacket paddled his canoe,
And three Thayers were hanged in open view,
    Was Old-time Buffalo!

Where savage life in the main prevailed,
Where approach was by Indian trail,
Then rail-trains met the gliding sail,
    Was Progressive Buffalo!

Where Great Lakes lay their tribute down,
Where miles of handsome homes abound,
And where its people own the town,
    Is Domestic Buffalo!

Where are rural parks and cosy drives,
Where shaded lawns in beauty thrive,
And massive structures point the skies,
    Is Picturesque Buffalo!

Where Niagara flows a rapid stream,
Where Nature's power replaces steam,
And bustling streets are smooth and clean,
    Is Excelsior Buffalo!

    Let zephyrs blow high or low,
        "Put me off at Buffalo."

www.ingramcontent.com/pod-product-compliance
Lightning Source LLC
Chambersburg PA
CBHW050450010526
44118CB00013B/1763